late summer ode

Also by olena kalytiak davis

The Poem She Didn't Write And Other Poems

On The Kitchen Table From Which Everything Has Been
  Hastily Removed (chapbook)

shattered sonnets love cards and other off and back handed importunities

And Her Soul Out Of Nothing

late summer ode

olena kalytiak davis

Copper Canyon Press
Port Townsend, Washington

Cover art: Painting by Augustin Kalytiak-Davis, courtesy of Olena
Kalytiak Davis

Copper Canyon Press is in residence at Fort Worden State Park in Port
Townsend, Washington, under the auspices of Centrum. Centrum is a
gathering place for artists and creative thinkers from around the world,
students of all ages and backgrounds, and audiences seeking extraordinary
cultural enrichment.

LIBRARY OF CONGRESS CATALOGING-IN-PUBLICATION DATA
Names: Davis, Olena Kalytiak, author.
Title: Late summer ode / Olena Kalytiak Davis.
Description: Port Townsend, Washington : Copper Canyon Press, [2022] |
    Summary: "A collection of poems by Olena Kalytiak Davis"—Provided
    by publisher.
Identifiers: LCCN 2022017847 (print) | LCCN 2022017848 (ebook) | ISBN
    9781556596476 (paperback) | ISBN 9781619322639 (epub)
Subjects: LCGFT: Poetry.
Classification: LCC PS3554.A93757 L38 2022 (print) | LCC PS3554.A93757
    (ebook) | DDC 813/.54—dc23
LC record available at https://lccn.loc.gov/2022017847
LC ebook record available at https://lccn.loc.gov/2022017848

9 8 7 6 5 4 3 2 FIRST PRINTING

COPPER CANYON PRESS
Post Office Box 271
Port Townsend, Washington 98368
www.coppercanyonpress.org

MIX
Paper from
responsible sources
FSC
www.fsc.org
FSC® C011935

to the great vowels A! and O!
my fruits! my flowers!
i love you(th) so badly!!!

CONTENTS

late summer ode

I Was Minor

In this life,
I was very minor.

I was a minor lover.
There was maybe a day, a night
or two, when I was on.

I was, would have been,
a minor daughter,
had my parents lived.

I was a minor runner. I was
a minor thinker. In the middle
distance, not too fast.

I was a minor mother: only
two, and sometimes,
I was *mean* to them.

I was a minor beauty.
I was a minor buddhist.
There was a certain symmetry, but
it, too, was minor.

My poems were not major
enough to even make me
a "minor poet,"

but I did sit here
instead of getting up, getting
the gun, loading it.

Counting,
killing myself.

[w]hat wond'rous life i[s] this [i] lead!
[r]ipe apples drop about my head;
[t]he luscious clusters of the vine
[u]pon my mouth do crush their wine;
[t]he nectarine and curious peach
[i]nto my hands themselves do reach;
[s]tumbling on melons as [i] pass,
[e]nsnar'd with flow'rs, [i] fall on grass.

(marvell)

a first pause in late [a]ugust, a first silence in early [s]eptember.

(nabokov)

Corruptive

The dark wood *after* the dark wood: the cold
after cold in April's false November.
In that second worser place: more gone, less there,
but in that lurid present present, cast and held,

rooted, kept, like some old false-berried yew.
Just against; the door leading to preferment
shut; no longer believing in *still*, by *some*, few
means, method, *could be*, but for the bad day set,

left, leaning atop bad day.

                                        Out- and un-

ranked, tooth-ached, wronged—ranckled corruptive thing!
Ill-wishing, in-iquitous, clipped, up-hoped, stripped: just plain: thin.
Dare thou commit: commit this final fatal sin:
God my God, I am displeased by spring.

And Then, Like

my late amaryllis
(tyranny of utter self-reflexiveness!)

exactly what was promised shows
arterial red

against the back-snow-light
of our long-black-winter-lives.

before the next season starts,
re-watch all of GIRLS

start with "the chicago train"
start with "the way things work"

watch this world unfurl
in order

(world gives you years,
years, venous and venial, opulent years—)

(yours did not follow, yours
trumpeted-not)

to make something of what is.
then, of what is left.

Decline

Both down and no. The mal de mer
of facing what's clear-
cut: these un-fine lines, the well-defined
slack and brace of time time time.

Glimpsed this etching first
in the summer of nineteen
ninety six: not possible; can no longer
fool: it's worn, it's ripped. Youth took this ship.

Youth hung on every fucking sail. Once,
sought south, sought light, sought
so low, to quicken and to slow.
Went too fast. Went too slow, some low flame

of having been. So many spots of sun, of sex,
and yet wasn't, didn't exist
on none of those days. Now
fading and waving: no, no, no.

Goes on too long. Too short. Over spent
and over wrought. So many and you want
them back? Such plain panic, such much
suffering stilled and still it returns---
but it is over over over.

Had my days and can not name them.
In the new nausea of nostalgia: will
have come to this. this. this.
this exact: moment of *is*.

On The Certainty Of Bryan

Bryan is ~~very~~ certain about the Ocean Park paintings of Richard
  Diebenkorn.
~~They are very good.~~
He does not have to say (or see) much more.
He especially likes the ~~almost~~ empty light blue one that is like
  an iceberg.
He also likes dense black and white photography, Japanese.
Not a soul, empty are the streets and houses he looks at/makes.
Yet people (have) live(d) there.
I guess I can see what he is not talking about, (we can both smell
  Lyana's ~~super~~ stinky feet), but I would be unsure or even left
  out without the certainty of Bryan. Bryan, should we have a
  drink? **Sure.**
Back in Alaska, I have opened the window to/on spring.
New ideas are breezing in, like students. I am: like students.

Did you read Eileen Myles's interview in that issue with the
  tongue
through/on the front? Despite my original skepticism, did she
  soothe me,
if only for a moment? I am completely unclear
on: my skepticism, ways, talents, dollars, "integrity," days, art(s).
  My life, it felt hard, hard, hard, hard, a little easier, fucking
  unbearable, hard, but was it?

Someone pretty smart was crying.
I did not know what to do.
"Now I'm tired and confused" I said, unable to tell what was
  going on
in someone (another someone) else's loins.
Then, once or twice, scared all afternoon of something that ended
  up
tasting: like baby food. Bryan has a ~~big~~ house in Brooklyn, a ~~big~~
  job **downtown,** a small child, a wife. His daughter goes to this
  little school **in a basement** in China Town. Eileen Myles might
  have passed them a year or two ago, on the way to fake beg.

Maybe if this was a short story the poignancy would hover in a
    short story atrium-y area,
maybe at the daycare/school and descend like light
on a certain mother or "wife." She is now a few blocks away,
    catching
her own reflection in that warn (**worn?**) warm mitt.
But why should I introduce any more characters?
We have Bryan, we have Diebenkorn, Myles, the **Japanese**,
    Bryan's kid and Bryan's wife. "We" have "me." Isn't that
    poignant enough?

There are mothers at the school and there are
    motherlikebutyounger teachers, but so far they all look the
    same. Yes, they have sick problems, but: This is not by Sam
    Lipsyte!

Oh, shit, Lydia Davis, yes, sure, if it's you, come in. Come in.
    Translate something from Dutch. And BTW WTF did you learn
    to speak/translate from Dutch?

I always am afraid to say "Dutch" and "the Netherlands";
Never "Holland"; rarely "de kooning," And is that *d* fucking
    capital or what? "One lip, tulips" and then they both laughed
    on my back deck cause
they liked each other so it was funny and of absolutely no interest
    to me, except here it is. somehow. again.

I have spent a month thinking about Bryan and his absolute
    certainty about certain paintings and photographs and how he
    matter of factly but quietly admitted that this certainty did not
    translate to his work. his life.
Do I know what I like
even a little?

I keep looking at the Diebenkorns online, maybe
wanting the book, which if I got I would forget to look at.
Supposedly he flew over a lot of stuff and liked how that looked.
Empty was the earth below, yet full of ~~lots of~~ people, no?

So I said/asked: Bryan, I am thinking maybe of writing a poem

about your certainty. What was the title of that Diebenkorn that
   made you start to draw icebergs?

Bryan says he will look it up after he gets home from work. He
   says:
I hope it has a happy ending.

Later he says: oh, that was John Zurier's *The Future of Ice.* Never
   heard of him, he says, absolutely unshaken.

Is there shit under my fingernail?
Is this meat I am feeding my children tainted?
When is the last time I had sex?

Meanwhile, Kary and I discuss the new *New Yorker* poem by
   Louise Glück.
She says: "I was waiting for you to love it to love it." and "I like
   how she rhymed 'precipice' with 'pillowcase.'"
I didn't notice (pang), but
I liked the relief tainted by the need to respond and I have also
   been meaning to say/ask:

that one Cave Singers song about getting younger? and
are you still flirting with Peter Richards online cause:
"After a while I came to know that death was the hay . . ."

Then, out of the blue, out of a southeast Alaskan clear blue-green pit,
actually, Dylan comes to visit, like some
traveling salesman of complexity. Jesus, he was
raised on a commune in Florida, he remembers the six buildings,
   the main dude who was some gay doctor, the way they had
   to sit and watch things burn, and he can see things before they
   happen
but what is happening that isn't, that brings him here looking for
   a friend in
patient and kind yet so unwilling "me"?
patient and kind yet so unwilling, "I"
meant everything, my seventy two hours of statements,

but:
so?

Back to nothing.
Suicidal panic.
I am broke and I am old.

Or I am still pretty
young and are these riches,
or fucking what?

and:

What did you think
of the poem with the mouse in it?
What did you think of the mouse?

Truth Procedure #1

Go to New York.
Stay with your friends.
Meet with your friends.
Drink with your friends.
Marijuana and cocaine with your friends.
Nobu with your friends and farm-to-table Chinese with your friends.
Zara and Uniqlo with one of your friends, your female friend.
Listen to your friends. All of them unhappy
with their girlfriends, wives, boyfriends, husbands, lives.
Two of your married friends want to sleep with each other, but don't.
One night you get really drunk and maybe do.
Sleep with one of your friends.
It's okay, you can forget about it, don't tell anybody.
It was and it wasn't awful. It was just stupid. It really didn't happen.
Another night you get really drunk and end up at a table of not
    your friends.
Even the loud (one quiet sexy) black dudes turn out to be boring.
Yes, you did and said stupid things in New York.
You know this pretty well, it is up in your throat and down in your
    stomach, but it is also already becoming hazy.
Next time, you will do better, make arrangements to meet other
    friends,
artist friends, different friends, less known friends, and
    see more art.
(You did go to Dia Beacon.)
Next time you will have more longer lasting memorable fun and
    discussions and really look at the art and not keep wondering how
    old you look, how dumb you are,
how broke, how alone.
Your heart will not ache at how they speak
to these girlfriends, to these husbands:
O familiar, I have just now forgotten to hate you. You will forget
    you forget you once had this. Next time
you will also prepare more effectively for your obligations, like
    lectures at NYU, so you don't have to re-give them repeatedly and

more successfully
in your head while you are running.
I mean, you didn't even use what you had.
It was supposed to be like an episode of *This American Life.*
You were supposed to start off with the quote from Keats's letters
that you were fingering for a while now: *I feel in myself all the
vices of a Poet, irritability, love of effect and admiration . . .* But
you couldn't do it, *and influenced by such devils I may at times
say more ridiculous things than I am aware of* cause Jhumpa
Lahiri and the Oscar Wao guy who you love but can't bring
up his name right now and wish he was sexier and better built
and then, maybe, with you, were all hanging there, in that back
room, and Jonathan Lethem was there next, really, Jonathan
Lethem next door and suddenly, your diatribe on the desire for
fame and accolades and the necessity of a life, a daily practice,
seemed wrong, too simple, too revealing of what you did not
have, of how little you learned in twenty years, *but I will put a
stop to that in a manner I have long resolved upon* how you can't
even tell if something uses a flexible hendecasyllabic meter *I
will buy a gold ring and put it on my finger—and from that time a
Man of superior head shall never have occasion to pity me, or
one of inferior Nunskull to chuckle at me* Who can? You were
supposed to tell them exactly how
you didn't get the grant you so needed to survive this summer.
     Exactly how the judges
were so stupid. Instead, you were stupid. are.
You faked it and it sucked. You sucked.
Now you know, now you know.
And each friend fit their form.
And each disappointed you in their own exact this-friend-that-I
love way. They can do it, why can't you? *I am certainly more
for greatness in a Shade than in the open day—I am speaking as
a mortal—I should say I value more the Priviledge of seeing
great things in loneliness than the fame of a Prophet—Yet here I
am sinning . . .*

Forty nine years to feel nostalgia,
fifty to get regret, these lines are for Rachel Zucker,
~~Deborah Landau,~~ Catherine Barnett.

All-Color

on one shelf:
all the white books I have read.
on another:
all the black ones I haven't.

they are leaning slightly, they
have liked my fingers, eyes, but they imagined better.

the first person I see when I walk out my house today,
if I walk out my house today, I will love forever,

we will use my entire bed and all my dishes, make dirty
each chair, shelf, drawer, cup.

and I will read to this late-determined love, aloud,
all the words in all the books with black covers.

then all the blue,
then all the red.

then, on a sunday, just like this one,
all quiet and mostly made of those four colors,
we will die, but only on the very surface,
knowing the many things we have not known yet.

De Mortuis Nil Nisi Bonum

This is how it played out:
not bad, not good.

I no longer love my own mother.

She has been dead that long.

I have earned this betrayal.
It was a long wrong done to me. And I
have betrayed others, but not quite
this soundly, this steadily, this well.

It is quiet. There is no argument in it.

The heart knows the mind simply can not.
It finds new love, new work—it chooses what to watch
and when no longer to be tender, careful.

I plant my pots, my children come and go:
they linger still as they outgrow me.

This is how it is; will not be.

Poem For Someone Stoned

(*whispered*)

it was all green
it was all green

or most-green
or green with what
embarrassed nature
likes to light

a fret of yellow
a purple mumble
to be perturbed
with white

and what it drank
and what it drank
before the sun came up

would happily do
the work of the poppy for you
bring you past brink
of a selvage so wide

past shadowy musk-rose
pine-line edge-trove
eglantine

and so the heavy hem of this
I lift

and so
the heavy
hem
of this

to give you cause
to ravel and become

to give you pause

to please

and so the sun
and so the sun

comes in
and out

of trees

back through the recent
field out past the dirty
flesh and violet veins

of leaves

behind
the callow furl
of fern

into the deep deep deep
sleep-dark summer
green

After Rilke

Dude, it is so done. Though Summer went on and on.
Now the shadows lengthen, now the wind spins. Gone.

Let the berries blacken. Let the fruit, over-
ripe, clot slacken rot.
Sober-up!
Still asking for—what? For more? Just two more
Hippocrene Days? Nothing stays,
nothing stays.

Too late to cove.
Too late to love.
Stay up read late rove stoned
through the now, the fast
raving leaves. Unraveling, last,
alone.

Late Summer Ode

Look, our little tree has taken root,
presents its fruit: thirty-six or -seven
ombré ways to cherry. Alone (and mute)
in the garden I garden, alone in
the garden, I crawl like a slow fly
over these books, I carry something out-
sized, something heavy and "literary,"
absurd and third, like an "act," like an overburdened ant,
alone in the garden, I Laevsky
my catalogue (un-)raisonné. I am so

Chekhovian: old sweater over old
underwear, shoddy, woolen, unkempt of
Ukrainian face, legs, hair, in the half-
kept tender-ly un(der) tended garden.
Like this: Like this, all summer, dishabille,
dishabille, at the table, in ruth's chair,
undistracted, able—yet—lacking act-
ion, thus, driven to distraction: (like this,
like this, I move to-ward: the form of form.)
something something something AND: o! there

's our new wasps' nest—good for one summer
only. All the rest the rest repeating
repeating: the sweet pea: revenant, re-
established shooting its florescence up
my late vacant trellis: REPEATING:
tender still and purple, purple. Some buds
to flower, some to leaf, from shade to sun
and sun to shade in search of a relief
that never comes: in my Vishneviy Sad,
sad, alone, just—holding—on: alea-
tory, asinine, like some old world pass-
erine, perched and panicked. and common.
common, the visitors come, and, (to some)

relief, the visitors go, altricial,
they say-sing, sing-said their made up songs:

Michaela came and told her story: I
can't stay in the house now that Grandpa wants
to have sex with me. Now that he can't re-
cognize me. Thinks I'm my dead grandmother
who raised me. She's twenty
seven, and met her boy-friend
online but, shhhhhh, she's already done
with him. She does not get along with
her mother. She says her little sister
is the shit: on fleek, but complains that
her sixth grade graduation eclipsed her
master's celebration. Me and Ruby
and Lyana and I listen. We watch
her whip, we watch her nae nae. Ruby
and Lyana stare at their more immedi-

ate future. Fletcher and his brother
arrive. They brought oysters. But right now,
right away they are hungry, hungry. They
eat the kale salad, the homemade bread,
the peach pie I baked, the Caprese
I made, wash it down with beer, white white,
Rosé, Rosé. They are from Juneau,
New Zealand, and Maine, because Richard's mother
gave him away when she was twenty
six or seven. Thirty or forty years later
he found his family. Now she's dead.
I can't understand a lot of what
'e 'aid: I can't see the resemblance, but,
they are, some version of the same. Ruby's here,

she's fourteen, here to visit her big-faced
bloated father. Ruby's shorts are very short. Her mother
is breaking up with her young
hedge-fund husband—oh wait—no she's not.

Ken was here a time or two, he's very
thoughtful, he brought halibut, he brought
"The Moose," so then I spent a lot of time
with, yes, again, Cal and Elizabeth.
I whispered this poem to herself. Pre-
cipitate and pragmatical. No.
Anomic and ominous. Yes. Auto-
nymous. Jonathan visited once. He
took an Instagram of the grapefruits'
orange squeezed rounds repeating round the pink
cutting board. Vodka. Vodka. Although we
hung out last summer, and I had wanted
to hang out more, (I did, it's true, / "he liked
you, then he changed his mind") (and couldn't get
it up) he now he lives with a pretty young
fat life coach and I was, i admit, a little bored.

Then Kary came. She's my Bishop, I'
m her Lowell. She magicked under
the tree with the green vine flowering
yellow from a red hanging pot round the blue
hula hoop; but she's starting to fade.
She's in constant chronic pain. She still tries
to groom it and tattoo it. Yeah, what are
poems and diaries for? Her young husband
read them the time before, last time she was
here, loves her and treats her well (despite the
un-unreversed vasectomy she sold
him from abroad). Yes, yes, yes. yes, the
visitors came, and the visitors went.
                    (and everyone I asked to leave—has left)

Back to my sole, my own alone: i proceed
by light, by shadow, by mirror
and by picture window: ow! and oh! and if
i write letters to my old lovers, I write(s) to them
from over there.
                    (Dear J, Dear K, Dear L, Dear M, Dear

N(!): remember the sex in LA? re-
member the times in lakes tahoe and
cuomo? remember that time in cassis,
in paris, in marseille?)

over here (dear Ch, Dear Jh, dear Bh), (in-
versely and in a lower key), it's all
less clear, like something other than a
painting and a painting: a flowering
orchard. a kettle of trees. under which
i self-protest, -process, and -recede. to-
ward an un-impaired despair. in a
picture bed! and on a picture chair! in
the garden, in the garden, (deceiving
elf!,) my passions watered, i moderate
my sorrow, by measure, number, and
by wait.

                    from person to idea and
                    idea to gate)

and yeah . . . yeah, that WAS woodthrush. and that was night-
gale, and that was Williams, (that was ashbery!?!) and that
    was Keats
(and that was some fine BULLSHIT) like a bird
it all repeats repeats repeats
until the mating's done. like this, like this:
i(t) moved from sun to shade and shade to sun:

it all happened, it all happened
i(t all) ripened, gladdened, slackened, saddened
and it happened the same way nothing happens
all of a sudden—alone in a garden—

The Benefit Of A Hangover

is pretty hard to discern
it is so not cool how you drank
that french cognac what did
you look like line-laughing your eyes
mouth open talking about
well,
your usual bullshit.
no one to cook you a bacon
cheese onion omelet
no one now someone
to hurt their feelings
(you will hurt everyone's feelings
everyone's feelings will
definitely be hurt) didn't you
just do this this last weekend
while you spouted ur alone shit
you were actually hurting two
people's feelings at once
wonder what is the record?
you said something like: just
this side of what is interesting?
did you? did you
call someone not interesting
by drawing that line: you are
nauseous and nauseated and
nauseating—go ago
regret everything.
did you talk about the form
you have not yet invented?
yes, you did
at least last night you
didn't mention dekooning
at least last night you
stuck to your druthering guns

everyone was american
and kinda french and
therefore eating with their right (left) hand
o sophisticatio
o lyric shame—what are you
asked the square art director
no one had read the knausgaard but me and tom
tom and i: the two artist-depressives
and he's usually such a dick
you look like carrie mathison though, ha, i am
solving homeland
issues right now: sorting
laundry later: dinner
no, it's pizza night
my children six feet tall
malnourished sugar addicted
i am a great mother
and my poems, my poems.

My Own Self Still Unconcerned

Lo, even as I sat in my under-
wear in brooklyn, in sweat and exist-
ential angst on a friday night so hot
so wrong (it was no "summer evening")

way way below the damasked* heights:
what did i ever(/e-ven) know of truth and light?
yea(y)(!), youth was gone and i was still as dumb
as shit. (but better ugly now!)

yet night how painful pure! i ate the white,
white shit, i did not call it "sustenance":
i stopped, i tried to look: the ache was coloured ochre.
baized and cornered, i could not (even) turn on the roku

(i) devised a grid
(i) shaded in one quarter
square (with ochre)
and dreamt on death and others 'lives
please. make fun of me(,) for how i suffer.

* prospect

Little Outdoor Poem

warm night warm night
can't quite see into
by someone's poollight
from the blackback window
of this huge stolen house

happy birthday to—
happy birthday—you
brooklyn alive with all
who have a special thing to do

downtheirstairs, i sit screened-in
on the porch after text-
arguing with my kids
about not taking care
of emily dickinson

warm nights! warm nights!
the neighbor's too loud
but pretty decent music
refinancing
the encroaching blue
magnolia

o subjectiveperceptualexperience!
my still warm heart sinks, sicks,
is heavy now,
is no longer high

as if, as though,
like, that,

i am just right now
sad with living
with (not) having
have lived

Poolhouse Plans

["WHAT'S UP, DETROIT?!"]

i have been thinking about the poolhouse
i have reviewed [in my mind's grid]
your ideas, and presentations, overall:
so many!

i think you really understand
where i stand on the poolhouse

the house and the poolhouse
[and, maybe, the BAUHAUS]

debating and thinking
i want to move forward
i want to move forward
debating and thinking

the one-level house instead of the three-level
the one-level

[the guest rooms on the basement level]

the one-level house is more "me"
                              more "me"
                    more "us"

we will use the house for ourselves alone
i will use the house for myself alone as well as with guests
as well as with guests [with guests, as well as]

a few comments and feedback

feedback feedback

feedback
the last floor plans

the last floor plans

we keep going back and forth
        over
        the last floor plans

in the denslashbedroom area north of the kitchen
in the denslashbedroom area north of the kitchen

we are leaning toward killing one of the bedrooms
we are leaning toward killing one of the bedrooms all together
we are leaning toward killing

we'd like to consider keeping
we'd like to consider keeping the bedroom at the top
we'd like to consider keeping   the top left

(so we would have a TVden AND a home office)
(so we would have a TVden AND a home office)
[TV then]

we feel the location of the current fireplace
we feel the location of the current
we like the idea of moving

we like the idea of moving the fireplace
        the fireplace
                            the fireplace

to the far west wall or on the wall
to the far west wall or on the wall
to the far west

wall or on the wall?
wall or on the wall?
wall or on the wall?

on the wall that shares
the dining room
                    the dining room

30

would be better served
better served as some kind of entrance
would be better served as some King of Entrance

to the terrace with doors
to the terrace with doors
to the terrace

near the master
near the master
near the Master

into the den
into the den
into the den[!]

design, materials, aesthetics
design, materials, aesthetics
we love the idea of having a private "garden"

we love the idea of having a "private" garden
we love the idea of having a "private garden"
we love the idea of having a "private"

design, materials, aesthetics
design, materials, aesthetics
we need to study having both the dining room and the living room

we need to study having both the dining room and the living room
we need to study having both

                              sunken

or just the living room
or just the living room
or just the living

as we spoke about
as we spoke about
we spoke about

a see-through fireplace
a see-though fireplace
a   fireplace

either way
either way
        way either

the entrance points
the entrance points
            points

to the large outdoor terrace dependent upon all this
the entrance points are dependent upon all this
            all this

and making that
                at a different level than the main
and making that at a different level than the main level

off the master
off the master
off of the Master

bedroom and bathroom
bedroom and bathroom
bedroom and bathroom

making the house three bedroom, three bathroom
making the house three bedroom, three bathroom
making the house: three bedroom, three bathroom

either way
dependent on this
dependent on this
either way

if we keep the plantings low, we think it will offer
if we keep the planting low, we think it will offer
if we keep the planting law, we think it will offer

privacy while maintaining the view
privacy while maintaining
        while maintaining

we'd like to see the chaise longues on the northern part of the pool
we'd like to see the chaise longues
                                        the view

we like the idea of an outdoor shower
an outdoor shower
an outdoor shower, as discussed, an outdoor shower

drawing that into the plan would be good
would be good to see how it fits in
would be good to see how it fits

a dining table at the west side of the pool
a dining table
another dining table

we'd like you to think of the fence
we'd like you to think of the fence
[the fence as opposed to the wall]

the wall, the fence,
the fence, the wall
we'd like you to think of the fence requirements

we'd like you to think of the fence requirements as part of this process
we'd like you to think of the fence requirement
we'd like you to think of the fence requirements

as part of the process, the fence requirements, rather than
as part of the process, the fence, rather than
rather than

it being an afterthought at the end
an afterthought rather at the end
and after thought at the end, after the end

we know we spoke briefly about this
we know we spoke briefly about this
only briefly about this [feedback]

but want to make sure
but want to make sure
but want to make sure the design of the fence

the design of the fence
the design of the fence
fence fence fence fence

is important to the overall look of the poolhouse
is important to the overall look of the poolhouse
            the fence is important

continuing the roof line of the poolhouse
continuing the roof line of the poolhouse
continuing the roofline

where the built-in BBQ is sited
built-in BBQ
where the built-in BBQ is sited

this allows for (i) more shade
this allows for (i) more shade
this allows for (i) more shade

if needed
if needed
if needed

and (ii) somewhere to sit if it rains
and (ii) somewhere to sit if it rains
and (ii) somewhere to sit if it rains

somewhere to sit if it rains and we still wanted to be there to eat
and we still wanted to be there to eat
and we still wanted to be there, to eat feedback

perhaps that roof can be partial
perhaps that roof can be partial
perhaps   partial

perhaps that roof can be partial solid roof, partial pergola?
perhaps that roof can be partial solid roof, partrial pergola?
perhaps that roof can be partrial solid roof, partial pergola?

we think it is something worth exploring
we think it is something worth exploring
worth, we think it is something

hot tub likely to be at the farthest south point
hot tub like to be at the farthest south point
hot tub likely to be

we'd like to have a small fridge
we'd like to have a small fridge
small fridge, sink, and 2 small dish-washing drawers

small
small
small amount

small amount of storage
a few glasses
and plates—not much

not much a small amount: not much
a small amount = not much
small

i think we need to study
i think we need to study
i think we need to study

i think we need to study the space
i think we need to study the space
i think we need to study the space

i think we need to study the space allocated
i think we feed to study the space allocated
i think we need to study the space allocated

i think we need to study the space allocated for these
i think we need to study the pace allocated for these
i think we need to study the space allocated for these

i think we need to study the space allocated for these items
i think we need to study the space allocated for these items
i think we need to study the space allocated for these items

i think we need to study the space allocated for these
i think we need to study the space allocated for these
i think we need to sutdy the place allocated for these

i think we need to study the space allocated
the space allocated
allocated

the space
the space
the space

i think we need to study
i think we need to study
i think we need to study

pool mechanics
storage spaceslashspace for pool mechanics
pool mechanics

we really want
we really want
we really want storage spaceslashspace for pool mechanics

underneath the poolhouse/deck
underneath the poolhouse/deck
underneath the poolhouse/deck

/
/
/

without getting nitty-gritty
without getting nitty-gritty
without getting nitty-gritty

-

-

-

we think these comments broad comments
we think these broad comments
we think these comments comments

we all agreed this can be worked into the slope
we all agree this can be worked into the slope
the slope of the land

we'd like to see the design develop
we'd like to see the design develop
we'd like to see the design delveop

around this concept around this concept around this concept
around this concept around this concept around around
around around around around

we love the direction this is heading
we love the direction this is heading so far
we love the direction this is heading

we want to keep the process moving
we want to keep the process moving

can you dimension out some standard specs?
can you dimension out some standard?
can you?

dash into the floorplan
dash into the floorplan

to see where they could go so we can
to see where they could go so we can
to see where they could go so we can

see how that space would function
x3

(iii) see if we have enough space dedicated
x3

we both think we should stop designing the main house
we both think we should stop designing the main house
we both think we should stop designing the Main House

for the time being
for the time being
for the time being

dive into the poolhouse
dive into the poolhouse
dive into the poolhouse

no pun intended
no pun intended
no pun

we were warned
we were warned locking down
might be difficult

we were warned
locking down a pool
contractor might be difficult

we were warned
we were warned
we were warned

might be difficult, even for next spring
might be difficult for next spring
might be difficult

next thursday evening would work
next thursday evening works for us
thursday works for us

works for us
works for us
work for us

we're excited!
we're excite to see this develop!
we're excited to see this develop!

we're excited
we want to keep the process moving
we want to keep the process

so we can finish the plans
so we can finish
                    The Plan

we think you really understand where we want to be
i think you really understand where we want to be
i think you really understand

where I want to be
with the house
                    and the poolhouse

let us know your thoughts
let us know your thoughts

let me know your fucking thoughts

The Analytic Of The Analytic Of The Panic

could not
sleep last
night

was dying of
an illness
was dying of
a sickness
was dying, dying
in a sick
panic

the numbers
of my life, my un-
paid taxes, the pain
in my
chest rising, rising
in my thick
throat
all night all night

"i" was diving, diving
"i" was all-night
dying

i tried to calm it,
to move beside it,
i(t) would not have i(t)
i(t) would have me

taxed
by death by panic

my death
my panic

used to pride self on:
"asked it, asked it"
for it was still
"the question"

but i(t) was noble
not last night last
time was when my tight
pants fit just right
last time was in a shower
of postecstasy when someone
pointed my face out to me

who will tell
the young?
who wants to warn
them? shall we
let them?

just
let them?

I Have Been

enervated, indigested. I defenestrated
i tried and followed. But I is restive, reliefless, with restless
legs. these are my symptoms, my poems.

the shadows of the shadow
of not something new, of no one's dog,
of not my cut-out hole-shaped soul.

no longer sex.
no longer food.

so cruel.

and no, please, no music.

so sorry, i tries to tell mylateself,

so sorry.

Today I Walked My Racism

today i walked my racism in a harness collar
through flatbush, through ditmas park
i called it buck, i told it to heel, heel, heal.

but i liked the houses on marlborough and rugby best
do you want to call it luck?
my hair was fake, but it was blond, blond, blonde,

i was blind, but not blind.
some guy yelled: *fine-looking pup!*
beautiful, like its owner!

just like its owner
just like an owner, owed, owned
i pulled and worried it; and loved.

Decorative Poem

Matisse. Matisse in his studio.
one two three four five six seven
lemons in the white bowl. one
outside it. the tabletop is pink;
the ledge of it orange. black red green
or blue green, if out the window.

Marya's lemons on her sills
one yellow two yellow three yellow four
her yellow hair and her apron, white and yellow.

Bryan's not-cut-out(s). he sold out
all his circles. he climbs the stairs into
the high-beamed-white. into the met, into the moma.

have you seen the light in
_____'s studio? that light.
there, all is order and beauty,
luxe calme et volupté.

the salmon geranium on the mexican-
blanketed table. its hot-pink stripes and the neon
pink candelabra. the ripening mangoes. six
all in the blue-hearted white bowl. redyellowgreen.
the ombré knotting in the window. from white to blue.
a little gold fox, a gold bottle, the fake 19th century
edelweiss in a small terra-cotta pot.
a thousand white and purple and rust pansies, waiting to be
hardened off, heartened, taken out

into the bright light of south of france, alaska.

Matisse is his studio. just now scrolling thru
the instagram. the rooms of it. the empty
rooms filled with it.

Hoarfrosted

what lack.
              what poverty, a poetry
that calls spade a white spade that calls
white branch after branch after branched.
forced crystal night-light: white.

white, like some hot-white nerve
was pierced, so together pieced
solid this comminuted crumble, this fuzz-
white space in place of place.
oblivion over oblivion.

don't say that word out loud!

              a simple cloud
came/went down. the inside of that cloud
was dumb-loud. was hard-shard white.
wan, was cold to coat this shit-
town. everything now overgone. went over

everything, in this day-lit-night, in sick-white know-glow,
        is missing.

My First Could

the first cloud i ever saw
was "saturnine"

i.e. it was a word

it did its bidding
its legal billing
like the poet-lawyer it was

these days, i can wait
sometimes

i can pause

can stay

can even ask for a continuance

i.e. i can still read a tony hoagland poem
full of joy and disdain

admiration and contempt
his clever cleverness me clevernesses

i want to say: o tony o poetry

again and again, because i swear
i did not choose you, you

i have always always hated you
more than loved you

and in this life i mostly left
"unrequited" to others

but i pined and hated
hated you

"chased"
"chaste"

because when you loved me
it was unlike any other love

you knew exactly how
smart and beautiful

and in what equal measure (!)

and you used me
exactly as needed

wanted loved
to be used

o tony,
towering vertical

are you now leaving me
alone with my top-heavy?

my first could

was a cloud

was a poem

A Grid, A Silhouette

i looked it up on wikipedia
derived from the name of étienne de silhouette
which i did after reading rebecca wolff's MSW application
which i did after drinking the not quite up to par latte
which i did after grinding the beans too finely
which i did while thinking of other other other things
which i did after shooting insulin
which i did after pricking my finger
which i did after waking up
after dreaming of sentences and logical structures
this this this contains not this and this
which i did after living an entire day in anchorage, alaska
alone with two relatively brief visits with each of my two children
which i loved because i realized i could do the same five things
   here i like
as in new york city where i will be in five days
and will have lunch at cafe cluny with joe
who will by then have recorded the first three or four sonnets
   in drag
and will have lunch at the century club with edward hirsch
who will by then have studied almost everything there is to know
   about Poetry
and will probably go to john derian and look up at the windows
above the storefronts on the bowery
and remember with pretty flat joy and pretty flat sorrow
other (non) times times times behind those windows
and creatures of comfort and no. 6 and my membership at the
   whitney and well
i will probably freak out as usual
several times at bryan's ditmas park mansion
realizing that his life is wrong
and my life has again been wasted
because all i did was, and in the cheapest way,

cut-out a person's appearance

Joie De Death

take this dread and flip it
on its bloody beak
think of how many times
you have already done this
on your moody bicycle
through the descending leaves

the sleeping lady now
sleeping now, covered with snow,
still whispering: it's yet to come. it's yet
to come. not now! not now!

the war on drugs—
that long new song—
reeling in and out

you will die before speaking
to your brother, but your son
will text him about wells fargo
fucking the once family
payment up

surely, you both hate that bank
and love the leaves these leaves

these green leaves leaves
that are yellowing and reddening
again this year

the fuchsia hangs on
the cosmos
the sweet pea—all the way up
the trellis—this year this year

how many times
have you resolved
to love this life?

now you must resolve
to love this dying.

dieter rams designed it!
and then there was le corbusier!

trying now trying now
you too will fail to admit it:

you were once on a streak
you died earlier this week

Here You Are

at natural pantry i discuss myself
while someone else's spit falls precisely on me
while the vegetables wait for me
while the vegetables wait

i could have been a contender
i will buy this little watermelon for my daughter
in coblenz in coblenz

the bends that's what i got each time it tried
to go forward to ride it out power through
i shall send you a paper bag full of sonnets
sometime to prove how everything everything is true

O Tempora O Mores

i stood in the line marked art-for-art's sake
then checked my self out yes of course there were
glitches in self-check out my first mistake
of something already in my bag was

unaware and it tipped the tiny scales
so i have a few religious friends one
republican i think they saved the whales
i think they love the overbearing sun

is catiline still not executed?
(scanning i had spied the paper rags) what
st. paul is left undeliberated?
wasn't there like a twelve page new york times article?

the chip plugged in my debit pin by rote
wait was this now the place to cast my vote?

In The Rick Yard

off the coach-road
with no gift for improving my luck

the nasturtiums
their leaves WERE pretty,
"what time IS it?" as i
loved to ask . . .

the chair fell thru the cracks
i sat on the wet spot
i stained the pelt with the juice of the fruit
i saved twenty dollars i lost fifty euro
thirty six cents

now i hated now i loved you
the time accounting statement
with its minus and its plus
its columns of calumny
went on and on and on

credit me
on this patriotic day
with my "dignity"
as i exercise my right
to "do not like"

o stupid stupid energy of words
all those summers i courted you
in tank tops and bikinis (in clogs!)
but i do not like you either

do not run thru me
do!
not!

who
who is making me

so UNCOOL!

making me
making me
always making me

write this one stupid stupid
stupid fucking POEM?

Vague À L'âme

when i am alone i am happy

it is the perfect temperature
inside my house the sky is
outside and the sky is
in: [i have framed your clouds]
the wallpaper behind it cloisteresque

nothing coy nor cloying and
success is always always far away

i have strayed
and stayed

because i love my dishes
i do not wish to die

After Chekhov

and before she slept
olena romanovna wept in earnest
it just got away from her
she wept mostly for herself
her already long life with all its painful and fruitless days

but also a little for her daughter

she did not weep for you

she woke here and there
in the slow snowlit night
to the flattening of her feeling
and noticed and thought on whether
that could mean "relief"

and in the still dark morning
olena romanovna woke in earnest
unsure of her catastrophe
but older and plainer still

The Death Of Ivan Ilyich

the mouse—or vole—
that lived/s? in my stove

stove off so much so so long

the sadness of

"arrangement/s"
"selection/s"

small readings

and the silence
in this province

gentlemen,
have you heard?

the pest gnawgnaws
at all my lovely lonely flaws

and as i already told the bosomed nurse
commeilfaut

(the very slightest of mental smirk/s
under my nose)

there is nothing
absolutely nothing wrong

with my heart
but my mouse!

(o vanitas!)
my vole! my vole!

Help In Spring

the snow snows light
and the snow snows quiet

i am still, i am even sleeping up there,
but i am pacing,
pacing

i whisk my ache, my lack,
my lacking

try and stop,
i begs of me
(try and stop!)
urges me
to bring my mother's
face to mind . . .

finally, finally,
her haircut looks at me and says:

poor solitary
little elephant,

trying so hard

Good (S)crap(?)

you know that pain i am always talking about
thinking about?

today it is in my
lungs

today is was

yesterday

disappeared in the rules of engagement

i re-arranged it
i painted over it
i bought it rugs and a pillow

did not sit
stood over it
stood to the side of it
stood way over there

i will store it in the blue refrigerator

i will clean it
i will sonnet and ode it

will plant it

under an unflattering
winter bonnet

lost it

heard the kitty in the litter
cover it

my life of it
(no)

Here It Is

the poem
that pretends it is suffering
as much as you

and truly, yay, truly
it does not know what to say
to whoever is calling calling ringing writing
to whatever is reaching
making small dumb sounds . . .

it ignores all
and with what cloud-glorious impunity!

excuse me, it thinks loudly, i am
a harried and haunted man!

right now, right
now someone is sending
another photo
of where the land scrapes
the sky, nay, the sea . . .

(how) could they be as lost as in need of
as me?

What Is Art

i wanted to follow
the ideals of the american high renaissance
but was hampered by my ukrainian
realism and corrupt technique.
i had once dated zelenskyy.
okay, he had once asked out me.
i was a perfect call, but, of course, of course,
no pressure, so said no.

i also once went with
liam gillick. he came
over and said today, today, i need to think
about what kind of dater i am
or still want to be. it was cute,
it was contemporary. we are/were
coequal and concomitant,
like luini and mabuse.

i too have abused my power.
but it was only powder.

poor me
always a madonna
or a bowl of fruit
always art informel

i informed on them when they were gone
said: don't know, beats me, but it sounded super smart.

This Table This Task

the illusion
of my humanistic leisure!

sketched a simple chair
and tried to sit it there

<>

now, having "written" ("you"?)
it sits

dismissed, unabled
by this table, this task

(skskskskskskskskskk)

Tolstoyan Weather

on our earth
you fell in love

with a mourning partner
someone in back

next to someone
with beautiful eyes

true, you saw a smile
light a dark velvet room

but you kept to your story, story
explaining something, sorry,
made of doom

"my door of my heart"
it was always heavy
over it, floated a painted cloud

this sadness now
a burgundy nostalgia
a bright blue nausea

it's okay it's okay
says the night under the night
and then, the grey-skied morning

Happy Birthday

want to have coffee in a romantical way?

it was the late seventies late eighties late nineties
i(t) was twenty twenty

my eyes were almonds
of light

i wore this
i wore there and then

the garden ukrainian
the raspberries red

we boiled everything
my awareness fizzled

on lawn chairs on the "big dock"
in green track shorts in white eyelet

off the shoulder then a dark prom-blue silky drape
and still i cackle and crepitate

mymothermotherinthecornerofmyeye
ormaybeitwasjusti

i can't remember, how long
how long ago was your hair?

back then then back

I Text Back

I am my own little monkey

***

and later:

***

I dare staid plaid

***

unattached

***

old in the mirror
young in the bathtub

***

that small dark thatch

***

wiping down
each leaf

***

of the domesticated ficus

***

fastforward
comes at me

***

no longer
an impossibility!

***

no longer
an absurdity!

***

my sexy sexy yes
i said
sexy

***

(TEXT IT!)
sixty-year-old-SELF!

Poemed

sky-blue-prison
prism of spin-back-earth

for fall is the time of damn-dappled,
of drab-drama-ed, of never-liked-
the-stubble-field-so-much-as-now

(and soon a roethke-complicated wait-light)

but now, now:
the yellow apples: appley,
crook'd, under the little-
armed tree

as yet un(h)armed by
the loud-littering clouds
slack-backing (back-slacking, slack-sailing) into town

ordered a new cerement
online

you look fine, fine! i said-said
to myself

then, like stephan trofimovich,
i made myself busy:

luckily, all the main characters
lived in my orange house

from room to room then!

corona, corona, i dylaned
as i made my chair, my desk, my bed
i sang (to myself, the most complex of all!)
where-you-been-so-long?

"did you make it love you can hear her"
someone not me wrote to a phone

Sonnets

i. (these now my glass)

ii. (you do not seem)

iii. (not stiff nor sharp)

iv. (these selves divided)

v. (not far from fair)

vi. (don't eat so fast)

vii. (so toned!)

viii. (individable)

ix. (who took my headphones)

x. (make an object)

xi. (my quietness)

xii. (i've put my hand to this)

xiii. (the threat of beauty)

xiv. (methought i saw)

xv. (do grow now)

xvi. (how long i longed)

xvii. (and then the quickening)

xviii. (this is what i am thinking)

xix. (on the self renewing edge)

i.

these now my glass now that my glass repels
these my fair my form and my reflection
my Two platonic forms they in spring myself
in autumn morn mourning my perfection

what triumph at what cost
did not grasp the what to whom contracted
but seeing plain that that i by winning lost
graceful transfer now must be accepted

having had these my having have now
look at them drenched in brightest shadow
they light my most ridiculous sorrow
once beauty had now my beauties follow

what but this envoy have i left to send
having rubbed off me it stuck on lovely them

ii.

you do not seem to realize beauty
realized must come from some other other
you but secondhand my lovely cruelties
i was first and before me my mother

i too remember one too old to ever
have bloomed full reached godly high snow
covered peak like this we minus sever
like from love refute known with what simply know

i most right was also wrong and now wronged
right my previous misconception
absolute did not long to me belong
i warn to alter you your perceptions

you took and took and took my all from me
my assets and my liability

iii.

not stiff nor sharp these my ornamental
cuttings from me the i without which
nothing loosen their visages gentle
go where gentle i proudly did bewitch

onlookers watch you not stand judgmental
that that beauty my beauty not resemble
i sit still in my beflowered mantle
just my pride not self but now parental

resent not form high spirit created
delight in loved likeness hair by hair
notice not what from what separated
mark human that which human this does share

fret not dears be but unsentimental
what was cut was made to disassemble

iv.

these selves divided from my selflessness
defect with consummate animation
go forth supreme superb superlative
less me than my masterly aberration

talented gifted and most polished
practiced perfected perfect ultimate
skilled skillful expert and accomplished
going rich gone gold beyond all estimate

and what poor have i left now that they have
left me a supplicant's hyperbole
i multiply what having had i halved
equation me with my metonymy

i math i count upon their countenance
they my argument and m'acquiescence

V.

not far from fair fair fell no longer i
but they but me writ more rare more varied
as far as i can tell we've hit the sky
dropped that fell that i long heavy carried

gained they what i lost for their very show
spring buds in wait of *summer evening*
and my decline tells all they need not know
lost in life now later's full gained meaning

thus having nulled superiority
my two subordinate propositions
away independent particularities
having late surpassed their one condition

beauty brought not what beauty thought i'd bring
i styled not One but Two enduring things

vi.

don't eat so fast stand up straight like this i
bred and warned those would too soon replace me
don't join any organized sport fuck crying
think only what you think no sophistry

they quick grew and quick caught what catch quickly can
one loquacious one cleverly silent
so both certain and terrifically unsure
(self doubt the sign of serious talent)

and so my two high truthful fallacies
go exploring into the exploding
world provoking doubt and duality
even as they prove my solid holdings

slow up accelerate o my alluvials
sit down be humbled sit down bitch be HUMBLE

vii.

so toned! intoned my daughter when she me
shirtless saw you still look good in a bra
and jeans (he too once said that (once) to me)
but i am done showing off showing awe

never proved enough for me i pronounce
me done AF renounce any sexual
pairing despairing not what i announce
gone having long been plenty plentiful

she strolls past demonstrating my better
once to me and he so swol so diesel
jacked and buff my form(s) did surely weather
now and now past both surpassing equal

means that not much this my most to me
so muscular your fucking sonnetry!

viii.

individable our canton spangled
with thrice repeating stars and hearts our catch
cry our left stroke just went viral dangle
provocation ask t'be met match by match

pentimenti leave o'er and o'er my mark
reinforce heighten prolong magnify
elongate enlarge raise swell boost protract
complement me supplement my supply

thus having repeated can retreat re
pair no longer consumed by my con
summation having twice brought full increase
sit fulfilled back and count and count and count

like this maximize i my written worth
most individable (there's levels to't)

ix.

who took my headphones my one working pair
snagged now likely snarled in your tangled teen
age shit leave my stuff alone don't you dare
those jeans still fit who went into my teem

ing purse pulled out the largest hidden bill
unflinching filched what was as not yet yours
and taking took my unmistaken all
unaware amateurs pinched all my wares

appropriated broad brow and even
broader shoulder seized my day unlawful
stole what yet seemed still in rightful reason
mine in still working order 'twas artful

wrong i am caesar's fra angelico's
noli me tangere you motherfuckers

x.

make an object do something to it do
something else to it like this i jaspered
my newly born materials into
brand new forms added heightened remastered

filled them with macaroni and cheese pop
culture we watched the throne bled on the tracks
are you STILL hungry rain drop drop top
"seriously mom can you fucking relax"

so neither direct representation
nor abstraction incomprehensible
autonomy above prior station
yet firmly stationed there indexical

i painted them after having dreamed them
my performance art my unearned income

xi.

my quietness has two babies in it
alone i am neither solitary
nor saturnine of them not thinking not
needing not yet no longer fragmentary

grown they have increased my valence i gained
by having lost and shared them compounded
am by their deeds more and less self contained
by their late astounding break unbounded

such is my valiance my gentle duel
between having been and having started
making kind what looks so awful cruel
thus having time once again outsmarted

it's ordinary it's optimistic
now sound now fucked dual atomistic

xii.

i've put my hand to this poem to these lines
just as i used to tend to my human
tending inclined to my fleshly vines
ensured circumstance for later blooming

took wide proved methods and my very own
confusion and hard wrought what my thought
had fast easy spun concepts unbeknown
untamed for wider purpose ignorant

i whipped and curbed thee my rough rhetoric
until i heard what meaning had to show
turned dictated madness's preference
away from clever toward the simple known

my minds and hearts so mad illiterate
but my hand kind caring and reverent

xiii.

the threat of beauty gone why do they ask
me not to come to stay away to take
my leave as if some part of fairest's task
was left to still some coarse deception make

or is this me reminder of that one
who took the breath from every sunlit room
who stole the hot glance of that very sun
that now puts on this self same state of gloom

ah jealousy was always someone's younger
sister with someone's sister's eyes and smile
and after her they always hungered
then asked that she make lovely gone a while

like this remembered i turn out to be
not by what lasts but long outlasted me

xiv.

methought i saw the figure of intellectual
beauty she looked a little bit like me
it wasn't necessarily sexual
but she was cool and sexy admittedly

she moved in ways that i had learned to move
she kindled process here and there she quenched
she spoke of finally being done with love
no longer longing that bright recompense

methought i saw in the corner of her eye
the thing thought that would be her eventual
doom the particle that would freeze the lake try
as she might to forestall the inevitable

so be it Unlove(d) now that we've come this far
there is a morning and an evening star

XV.

do grow now as they grow less young younger
until we contemporaries be i
not just slowly counting my new numbers
but newly one with what i multiplied

we all like chance right and marijuana
and karl ove david foster wallace
kendrick definitely still nirvana
kafka getting into fucking college

our ignorances and our biases
quite similar shit i too long to quit
but we go along our strong compliances
to some master's master plan counterfeit

what when our one and only life proves ass
keeping it all one hundred puff puff pass

xvi.

how long i longed for one enduring thing
something sculpted in indestructible
stone alone i worked toward that something
noticing nothing inexhaustible

made attempts through pure renunciation
sought out trance and dreamed of true transcendence
met only frustration and negation
lost all will but still willed coalescence

grave paralysis thick self estrangement
of those two substances was all i made
'cept the two of flesh those fresh arrangements
who now present as best that i portrayed

turns out these my reifications be
i le(f)t them loose for all the world to see

xvii.

and then the quickening of melting spring
which i do count in terms of what lies left
no longer an abundant offering
but one less the original bequest

how many more first looks at firstest bud
how many lasting days of waxing hope
how many new seeds new causes new loves
how newly limited my scion's scope

o to generate more inflorescence
originate ovule that none do expect
show more than berries of my conceptions
tree more increase outdo my rudiment

o sweet smelling nucleus i praise thee
i have lived in wait of thy bright poesies

xviii. (this is what i am thinking)

methinks i lied all winter when i cursed
my lack of purpose said i had nothing
left hard cried my grey white blight nursed
my moan bemoaned my abusive stunting

but as ever promised spring does undo
winter's harsh relentless banishments
so does this season prove me extra new
unestablish my disestablishment

what rested dormant now shows zoetic
pushed through to industrious restorement
so i stand healed fired reerected quick
fresh preferment's most willing applicant

thus my wasted wit's new versant teeming
thought mind dead asleep was forceful dreaming

xix.

on the self renewing edge of my own
departure too chose brutal beautiful
ruination ineluctable now
wear all white await th'inevitable

no longer ask what my verse can bring me
just diligent scan what late was scanted
record record of blank identity
the certain light now serious slanted

but what so sicked no longer pains and scars
lose their blistered denotations eclipsed
the once marked fixed despairs those bright blue stars
from the new skyscape scraped erased dismissed

that once proved false soon too false proven be
new life kills all and will kill dying me

xx.

i know that i am wrong when i present
my disappearing presence for ne'er did
mind nor sight full glean my certain content
'stead artful blurred what underneath lie hid

so quested faultless flawless curt surmised
what longer narrative did long to tell
made story short and simple prized
disguised o'er what inside did unterse dwell

decay now reveals most darkened hardened
surface fucked insides tough and marvelous
where is ted berrigan when you need him
bellowing upstairs "come fuck me alice"

in some other room we destined be to meet
we'll not count meters' syllables but feet

xxi.

limbeck alembic what do you call that
drink i drank when i did slowly drink of
you it avails me not t'taste from my mouth
gone long dispersed proof of no more of

altered state unaltered equaled straightened
final cause ungained from first causation
became my own steady inestimate
planisphere without new application

i suppose i never will love again
having tasted that after after taste
nonetheless someone come with me to spain
still beautiful unseen seems such a waste

bother not with your etiology
it's metaphysics not biology

xxiv.

i know the alteration that is love

XXV.

mored this downplayed that vanity was my
taskmaster my tastemaker all that while
made myself more beautiful but did not try
to make you my poems any wilier

i took you as you were i let you stand
in worstest light in most terrible truth
showed you ugly off as if my hand
had barely touched what i did introduce

sarah burton for alexander mcqueen
a nude embellished gown long long long torn
both frayed and embroidered and in between
what is still extant and beautiful gone

count now and color in the quiet in
a fragrant single stalk of hyacinth

xxvi.

not what i feel now for my son but what
my mother felt for my brother not me
not beautiful daughter not selfsame but
shining son so tall so strong so kindly

that is where a mother's heart finds new rest
she can not help it it sores toward that
exact height of him her first born her first
what joy to her earth finally granted

i should have let her have it him i did
i turned away and found my own own men
how quickly they disappointed then lived
it out until it got what wanted then

this month it will be five years since we spoke
twenty thirteen that year i was so broke

xxvii.

in the poem a window in the window
a mountain on the mountain the sun on
snow which melts in white diminuendo
everything until now and now now on

depression is for the young o how i
did drag through all those years the crazy of
my face with no joy two little kids i
crossed streets climbed hills and italy and love

now i make authorized payments i read
sheila heti like candy like eti
ology in two thousand nine she stole
it all from me motherhood didn't she

i have the instant message to prove it
my relationship with nam the conduit

xxix.

my tall son comes by to discuss nothing
everything he finished the nabokov
i left on the stairs we discuss nothing
everything coltrane was really drunk

last night stoned people are mostly really
sad i still want a real house on some real
land and to write one small enduring thing
that's not that unrealistic well

except for the one great thing did zadie
write it no franzen no david wallace
poor thing my friends think you are in your thirties
he packs nabokov's lectures and he leaves

relieved i go out for my six mile run
there is a little rain first then the sun

xxx.

(the iamb and the anapest the dac
tyl and the trochee the right words in the
right order by instinct if you're lucky)

xxxi.

i fucking glazed it; olena kaly
tiak davis from anchorage made this!

xxxii.

my aloneness bound(ed) my their arrival(s)
(and yet) a stunning and suffered survival

xxxiii.

let none look and not see these new lines
not much, how bout you? i'm doing fine

erased sonnet

lack
stone
slack
bone
tide
receptacle
bide
spectacle
untoward
safe
bored
late
true
true

sonnet for mark, joe, ted

or maybe a sonnet-novel! (i've had
an idea or two in my life . . .) streets
of brooklyn, new york: what am i to you
but a still refreshing drink of seawater?
an old friend not seen (in the interior)
for thirty years for thirty years saw
everything! it all lies there inside-out-
him. berrigan, because what is under-
neath the words: those days: a casual
causality, a caring casuistry
that eases me. thank you for my new life plan.
i relax with you, ted, speaking much quick,
i who have never relaxed taking inventory
of face body brain pulse taken over

and over again: hello, dear otters, hello.

airless sonnet

you still in it in order to order
check self against nonself, against nonsense
nothing hurts   there's no pain-stitched border
tween how-torn internal and the suspense

of the "ex-," of the "e-," of the "di-"
o enormous discrimination, what
intended was very far from here, from i
a moment of of, a small self-portrait:

the chair squeaks like a child i am done with
it frizzles, my hair, though i it want
smooth: through the thick, the thick thicket unwit-
tingly, airhurt, and with prodigious lack

of purpose . . . find myself making certain (marks) in it
in this still interim, 'tween what and not

Chekhov, Baby

Brus Kennetovich came round the back of the orange house
carrying some sort of camera bag and a bottle of A to Z pinot noir.
It was moving to the end of September, and the tulips were
already planted in Olena Romanovna's back garden. The dirt over
them grey, black, and still wet with a three-days' rain. The flow-
ers had come and gone during the now-long and almost long-ago
summer, but not all. The large trellis, attached to the house—
not like a modernist grid but like a huge dumb tic-tac-toe—and
usually still alive with the leaves of the pink and purple sweet
peas, was empty. As was Olena Romanovna's heart.

Brus Kennetovich was wearing his usual cap. As always,
it said something about art and society and/or a new project
Brus Kennetovich was currently working on. He wore a white
sweatshirt with the words TRAILER BUILDING SUPPLY and
black track/sweat pants with the adidas stripes and even the word
adidas, although writ pretty small, and his feet looked small in
his odd sporty laced-up sandals. There was a black bandana round
his neck because of the current plague, which had reached all
the provinces, even this one, which was very far north and where
people were very far away from the world and each other, usually
alone with their various and highly specific contagions. He wore
dark socks and had on dark glasses. Olena Romanovna decided
not to put on her dark glasses, which she did have at the ready,
and which she usually employed at even the glint of a possible
social interaction, indoor or out, day or night, because they made
her disappear. But she did not want to feel silly for the next hour
and a half, two, looking through her glasses into/at Brus Ken-
netovich's glasses. Brus Kennetovich had barely spoken when she,
with her old dark eyes (dull, dull, but still set at a compelling
angle), first started wondering when it would be over, over.

Brus Kennetovich amiably answered questions about his
children. His oldest, Sara Brusova, was living in a more southern
town in the province, was on the cusp of forty, and had just had
a new baby. (A boy, her second born, Silas Danylovich, as was

the subtle old-new fashion.) (His big little sister was Nora, was Nola.) Sara Brusova was a therapist who had once live in The Great City. Brus Kennetovich had always been close to her, his firstborn (he had been a young father by the current standards of the educated, who now delayed and delayed the inevitable, but, of course, still knew nothing), and a "life coach" for her, but Brus Kennetovich reported that the tables had started to turn, turn, and sometimes, he sought his daughter's counsel.

His son, Gabe Brusovich, was living in the same town where the two interlocutors sat, shit-talking it and most of its inhabitants, themselves, of course, excluded. Not only had the town not improved over the last twenty years, Brus Kennetovich agreed, it had, in fact, gotten worse. This was mostly due to the unimaginative behavior of its "leaders," whom Brus Kennetovich knew personally and were, he attested, not very smart. They could only be "leaders" "here," in the largest town of a remote province. Gabe Brusovich, his only son, was not of their ilk, of course. A young builder and "perma- . . . um . . . lander?"—the exact term escaped Brus Kennetovich's mind, but, obviously, a special more thoughtful and kind lover of and liver on the land, the same land he had been born to some thirty some years past. The very land and mountains, mountains, mountains, that were, at this late moment, turning orange with pride and love. (Later Olena Romanovna would text-ask and Brus Kennetovich would text-answer: "perma-KULTURA.")

Sofya Brusova, Brus Kennetovich's youngest, was a lawyer in a larger, currently hip, small city in another western province, clerking for a federal judge. She had taken time off "to be a young person," and, as a result, had now found her correct vocation. Protests in the hip small city were the talk of other towns, but Brus Kennetovich and Olena Romanovna knew each knew all there was to know and discussed it no further. What was there to discuss, the police needed to be defunded—at least in some "right" way—but would not be. All would continue as it was and had been since time immemorial (or at least since the non-emancipation of the serfs.)

107

All was well, well, with Brus Kennetovich's children, and Brus Kennetovich could now, at his own ease, study the current global climate, the actual climate, the pandemic, and fight for minority rights. He told Olena Romanovna that it was an exciting time in his mind, and he woke up every morning wondering what would happen next. He was no longer suicidal.

As for himself (—the current art project we will discuss in a moment or two—), Brus Kennetovich had a new "five-year plan." This plan had involved an apparently light-hearted calculation of Brus Kennetovich's life span. Based on Kenneth Borisovich and Anna Ignatovna, i.e. his father and his mother, he would live to seventy-nine. Eighty tops. Each of his parents had perished at that exact age, though each from different cataclysmic bodily events. Brus Kennetovich's "five-year plan" was one year in. It would take Brus Kennetovich another four years to save up enough money for his final ten, which he would spend "traveling." This travel would involve "visiting," i.e. "staying" with, various personages, including his older brother, with whom he was also close, close, and who lived in a dry rural province not far from where the family originated. The older brother and his wife, who had already started "traveling," had both been schoolteachers.

He had been talking for some time, when Brus Kennetovich removed his dark glasses. Was the sun really lower, or was it momentarily behind the neighbor's red shed (which had, of course, been converted into an overpriced rental)? It was not an entirely stunning reveal. Olena Romanovna already knew of the large, heavy bags under Brus Kennetovich's sixty-five-year-old eyes, and had noted, on several previous occasions, though most now years, years ago, how extraordinarily sparkly, doelike and feminine Brus Kennetovich's actual eyes were. Yes, they were still and again an unusual sight.

The current art project, Brus Kennetovich finally/now explained, was a simple idea, but complex in execution. It involved eight northern kingdoms. The plague with its travel restrictions had obviously slowed the already leaden process.

The idea was that in the northernmost towns of these northern-most kingdoms would be installed eight "boxes" with "phones" inside them. So, at any time someone entered a "phone" "box" they could, potentially, pick up a "phone" and communicate with whoever else in whatever other kingdom was also in a "phone" "box," and had also picked up the "phone." Each kingdom could invent the style and composition of its own "phone" and "box." The project was called EIGHT BOXES, although the kingdom of Tolstoy and Dostoevsky, of Gogol and Turgenev and Pushkin and Gorky, and yes, of Chekhov, wanted eight boxes all of their own. They were convinced of the error of their thinking by some architectural firm or maybe some radical artists. It got blurry for Olena Romanovna (as it often did) and/but the project remained discrete: eight boxes in eight kingdoms. Next time he came over, Brus Kennetovich would bring photos. The one in this kingdom, in the interlocutors' shit town, would be at the corner of 4th and E. Olena Romanovna tried to picture that exact corner. Although the heart of the shit town, and 4th and E, was just a couple blocks from Olena Romanovna's house, and although Olena Romanovna did a lot of aimless walking, that exact intersection escaped her. She did know the corner of 3rd and F.

Greenland was a wondrous country, said Brus Kennetovich. Everyone everyone everyone was Native. Nuuk was the capital. The town was small but felt huge, or maybe it was huge and felt small.

But Olena Romanovna was on the phone. She had picked up a phone in a box (Dolce & Gabbana had designed this one, but it was definitely not in Italy) and dialed NAM12345678, and was waiting for an answer. She noted that she was not at all nervous, although at least ten years had passed since she had last spoken with her young, much younger, lover. Her mind skipped over times and arguments and bathrooms and cities. Their romance had been quite a whirlwind: it involved Saratoga Springs' swimming pools, a swimming hole near Lake Tahoe, LA rooftops, Italian bathtubs and Italian gardens (maybe that's why the D&G). In fact, much of their unreality had unfolded in real life at a villa at Bellagio. It involved a balcony far below which Lake Como reflected cloudless (or gentle-clouded) Italian skies and lapped at Italian (and Swiss?) mountains.

In order to be able to stay at the villa in Bellagio with her young lover, her young lover had had to lie to the Rockefeller Foundation and say that Olena Romanovna was his "life partner," even though they had only been "together" for a couple months, and most of that at a distance. The young lover had in fact felt he could not get any "purchase" on Olena Romanovna, despite her prominent hip bones. Surely the reams and reams of Google Chat were proof of something.

Every late Italian afternoon they drank French champagne and ate American bbq potato chips and did, indeed, make love. One afternoon an Italian maid walked in on them. The young lover, who was nothing if not a studied and exceedingly polite and erudite young man, had stopped midthrust and said something polite IN ITALIAN about being busy. The door closed and they laughed and laughed and fucked and laughed.

At "Bellagio," everyone was expected to dress up for dinner every night. Olena Romanovna was especially good at this, and was wearing, to this particular Tuesday-night celebration of another dull scholarly and/or artistic day, a short rust-colored bubble-shaped dress with a gold halter neckline (a knockoff of a Jennifer Lopez dress she somehow knew, but still a knockout, flattering, flattering), and highly flattering (Italian!, but purchased online) thigh-high black boots with tasteful zippers and exactly the right heel height. Some short-haired plain-faced law scholar had commented: "I wish I could wear boots like that!" and Olena Romanovna, looking modestly down yet slightly raising her right toe answered: "You can! You should!" Her face and form complimented each other as if saying: "You first, no, you . . ." (As Olena Romanovna and her young lover had walked down the long Italian carpeted hall to perhaps this particular dinner (—no, I think she was wearing a short, sexy, sleeveless black dress with an Audrey Hepburnesque or priestlike white collar—) her young lover had in a soft, even voice told her that that was, in fact, the best head of his life . . .)

After dinner, a Dante scholar, an older-older woman, maybe a grandmother, wearing something that no one would ever comment on or covet or remember, had recounted this nonencounter:

"I was walking in the garden
yesterday afternoon," she said,
"and I heard voices.
"I could not tell where the voices
were coming from
and I could not hear
what the voices were saying,
but the voices were engaged
in 'conversation.'"

She met each of their eyes.
"It was the two of you,
on the balcony.

"A back and forth.
"A quiet conversation."

Olena R. remembered how unhappy she had been at "Bellagio" with the level of conversation, of sex. She had made a scene or two inside the beautiful Italian room. In front of its large gilt mirror, on its large white bed, lying on her back, staring up at the Italian ceiling . . . But on that balcony overlooking Lake Como—in just a bra and tight tight tan corduroys—smoking a cigarette, three, actually reading or maybe just holding, folding back, PARADISO, the words above or below or beyond understanding— . . .

Olena Romanovna, still holding the ornate and colorful receiver, felt her heart. It was full of nausea and regret. Her heart was the very heart of the D&G design probably named "Nostalgia." She would never again be smoking, disconsolate, on that paradisiacal balcony, and that balcony was the very apex of her life.

At not 4th and E, Olena Romanovna put the phone down, before her young—no, now no longer so young, now maybe forty-year-old—lover could make the choice of whether to answer or not.

Olena Romanovna noticed the emptiness of Brus Kennetovich's heavy pink cut-glass glass and asked Brus Kennetovich if he wanted more and Brus Kennetovich said "Yes."

Olena Romanovna went inside and squeezed more grapefruit. The counter was sticky and messy with many half rinds and pulp. She made herself another strong one. She was not drunk at all. She went back past the music, outside, into the slow quick fall.

When she handed Brus Kennetovich back the heavy nonalcoholic glass, Brus Kennetovich spontaneously explained why he was not drinking. It was last autumn, while traveling for the selfsame project he had just described. He found himself sick in a faraway hotel room. Five or six days passed and Brus Kennetovich started to think he was really dying. He went to bed on that sixth night resolving that if he did not feel better in the morning he would go directly to the hospital. And when he woke up on that seventh day, Brus Kennetovich now looked at Olena Romanovna with his bagged girlish eyes and held up a forefinger and a thumb, not very far apart. "I felt that much better." Five or six more days of illness had followed, and he traveled home and had not had a drink since. Brus Kennetovich drank down his second freshly squeezed grapefruit juice in the heavy heavy glass.

Olena Romanovna asked and listened, listened and asked. She probably added things about her own situation, family, life, that was right there (was it still?) in the orange house behind her, which had music seeping out of it, a Spotify mix made for her by her friend Kevin Jimovich, and a table lamp or two already lit against the darkness, the darkness that would be here soon, soon. And Olena Romanovna did not look at her watch, which was an "I"-watch and dinged every so often and then not, because she forgot how to silence it and did not have her real glasses, and drank her vodka and grapefruit slowly, slowly and did not feel its effects at all, and wondered if she had mistakenly given Brus

Kennetovich the glass with the two or three shots. Olena Roma-
novna wondered how much longer. The sun was close to setting
and the wind blew the yellow and brown leaves about in circles
on the still-green ground and made the green leaves on the trees
frantically wave: goodbye, goodbye.

And at some particular point, now long into the conversa-
tion (was it a conversation, was this what a conversation was like
in the province?), Brus Kennetovich's phone rang and he found it
and looked at it fleetingly and silenced it and put it in his pants'
soft pocket. He asked if it was okay for him to smoke one last
cigarette, before he left.

About the Author

Olena Kalytiak Davis, a first-generation Ukrainian-American, was born and raised in Detroit and educated at Wayne State University, the University of Michigan Law School, and Vermont College. This is her fourth full-length collection. Her first book, *And Her Soul Out Of Nothing* (University of Wisconsin Press, 1997), received the Brittingham Prize. Kalytiak Davis's honors also include a Rona Jaffe Award, a Pushcart Prize, and a Guggenheim. Kalytiak Davis lives in Anchorage and Brooklyn.

Poetry is vital to language and living. Since 1972, Copper Canyon Press has published extraordinary poetry from around the world to engage the imaginations and intellects of readers, writers, booksellers, librarians, teachers, students, and donors.

COPPER CANYON PRESS WISHES TO EXTEND A SPECIAL THANKS TO THE FOLLOWING SUPPORTERS WHO PROVIDED FUNDING DURING THE COVID-19 PANDEMIC:

4Culture
Academy of American Poets (Literary Relief Fund)
City of Seattle Office of Arts & Culture
Community of Literary Magazines and Presses (Literary Relief Fund)
Economic Development Council of Jefferson County
National Book Foundation (Literary Relief Fund)
Poetry Foundation
U.S. Department of the Treasury Payroll Protection Program

WE ARE GRATEFUL FOR THE MAJOR SUPPORT PROVIDED BY:

TO LEARN MORE ABOUT UNDERWRITING
COPPER CANYON PRESS TITLES,
PLEASE CALL 360-385-4925 EXT. 103

WE ARE GRATEFUL FOR THE MAJOR SUPPORT PROVIDED BY:

Richard Andrews

Anonymous (3)

Jill Baker and Jeffrey Bishop

Anne and Geoffrey Barker

In honor of Ida Bauer, Betsy
  Gifford, and Beverly Sachar

Donna Bellew

Matthew Bellew

Sarah Bird

Will Blythe

John Branch

Diana Broze

John R. Cahill

Sarah Cavanaugh

Stephanie Ellis-Smith and
  Douglas Smith

Austin Evans

Saramel Evans

Mimi Gardner Gates

Gull Industries Inc. on behalf of
  William True

The Trust of Warren A. Gummow

William R. Hearst III

Carolyn and Robert Hedin

David and Jane Hibbard

Bruce Kahn

Phil Kovacevich and Eric Wechsler

Lakeside Industries Inc. on behalf
  of Jeanne Marie Lee

Maureen Lee and Mark Busto

Peter Lewis and Johnna Turiano

Ellie Mathews and Carl Youngmann
  as The North Press

Larry Mawby and Lois Bahle

Hank and Liesel Meijer

Jack Nicholson

Gregg Orr

Petunia Charitable Fund and
  adviser Elizabeth Hebert

Suzanne Rapp and Mark Hamilton

Adam and Lynn Rauch

Emily and Dan Raymond

Joseph C. Roberts

Jill and Bill Ruckelshaus

Cynthia Sears

Kim and Jeff Seely

Joan F. Woods

Barbara and Charles Wright

In honor of C.D. Wright,
  from Forrest Gander

Caleb Young as C. Young Creative

The dedicated interns and
  faithful volunteers of
  Copper Canyon Press

The Chinese character for poetry is made up
of two parts: "word" and "temple."
It also serves as pressmark for
Copper Canyon Press.

The poems are set in Marion and Avenir.
Book design and composition by Becca Fox Design.